The micro theology series scratches an important itch: accessible books addressing crucial topics. And Jonathan Foster is the ideal author for this series. What a fantastic way to explore what matters most!"

—Thomas Jay Oord, author of *Open and Relational Theology* and other books

Jonathan invites us to imagine a God whose love is so compelling and relentless that, in the end, we are wooed—not threatened—into surrender.

—Loren Richmond Jr., Chaplain and Ministry Consultant, host of the *Future Christian Podcast*

Jonathan Foster unpacks the "why" behind shifting views on hell with a compassionate mix of honesty, depth and solid research. This will help so many people who are wrestling with big questions in a way that is both evidence-based and relatable.

—Leslie Nease, author of *Honoring the Journey: The Deconstruction of Sister Christian* and Host of *Honoring the Journey Podcast*

This is not simply another boring "hot take" on hell. Instead, Foster offers a deep, honest, and human analysis of how Love screws with our tired conceptions of who's in and who's out. Love, it turns out, is more difficult than fear, retribution, and wrath. Are you up for the challenge? If so, let Foster be your guide!

—Josh Patterson, host of *(Re)thinking Faith Podcast*

Love Burns Like Fire

An Open and Relational Take on Hell

Jonathan J. Foster

Copyright © 2025 by Jonathan J. Foster

All rights reserved. This book or any portion thereof may not be reproduced or used in any manner whatsoever without the express written permission of the publisher except for the use of brief quotations in a book review or scholarly journal.

NO AI TRAINING: Without in any way limiting the author [and publisher's] exclusive rights under copyright, any use of this publication to "train" generative artificial intelligence (AI) technologies to generate text is expressly prohibited. The author reserves all rights to license uses of this work for generative AI training and development of machine learning language models.

Paperback: 978-1-968136-28-4
Ebook: 978-1-968136-09-3
Audio: 978-1-968136-10-9

Printed in the United States of America

Library of Congress Cataloguing-in-Publication Data
Love Burns Like Fire: An Open and Relational Take on Hell /
Jonathan J. Foster

for my sisters
lifelong friends
and the best of listeners

Table of Contents

Micro Theology Series Introduction............. 1
- Love is the Lens......................... 3
- A Working Definition of Love.............. 4
- I Believe in You......................... 6

My Context..................................... 11
- Open and Relational Theology 11
- Mimetic Theory 12
- My Lived Experience with Three Inciting Incidents................................13
- Now You Know...........................19

Love Burns Like Fire: An Open and Relational Take on Hell 21
- What Is Chunking and What Does It Have to Do with Thoughts on Hell?...............21

- Never Abandoned by Love 22
- I Changed My Mind About Hell When I Realized 24
- Take My Punishment 32

Some Comments from the Original Essay on Substack/Patreon............................. 35

A Few Resources................................ 55

About the Author 57

Some Other Books in the Micro Theology Series 59

AI Disclosure 61

Micro Theology Series Introduction

Book 2: Love Burns Like Fire

There's an old story that my friend likes to share about a woman who wanted to translate and distribute the scriptures to her community. For several years she saved her money until she had enough to pay someone for the translation. Just then, a pandemic hit her community. With her neighbors suffering and even dying by the dozens, she decided to spend her money on medicine to care for the sick.

Eventually, the pandemic ended, but not before it exhausted her savings. For several more years, she worked diligently until she once again had enough to pay for the translation. But then a famine struck.

Friends and neighbors were on the verge of starvation, so she took the money and bought food to keep them alive.

When the famine ended, she was broke. So, she started over. As she grew older, she saved every penny. Finally, at the end of her life, she was able to get the scriptures translated and distributed to her people.

For the remainder of that community's existence, whenever that story was told, someone would point out that the woman had translated the scriptures three times throughout her life . . . and the first two were the most powerful.

I love that story, and whatever I have to say about theology or one's approach to the bible can't be said better than what it communicates. It's probably apocryphal, but whenever I hear it, I recognize truth. The depth of truth is more than just a set of propositions lined out and bullet-pointed. The depth of truth is a relational movement motivated by love. Whatever spirit you sense from that woman—whatever matrix of reasoning she used when faced with those difficult choices—that's the point. Honestly, that's it. To add more words, micro-expression or not, is to risk getting off track. So, you should probably be careful with what follows.

Love is the Lens

The micro theology series is "micro" in word count only—these topics span a wide breadth of theological inquiry, presented in accessible, Substack/Patreon-sized reflections. My goal is to help you, the reader, engage theology through a lens marked less by closed minded dogmatism and more by open-ended reasoning. Which is to say, I hope to help you fashion a lens of love. This is not only permissible; it's what the bible with its undeniable interest in powerless nations, scorned victims, and scapegoated saviors, encourages us to do.

Note: this isn't a lens-free approach. Such an approach doesn't exist, for none of us comes to a text outside of a *context*. Context is informed by a variety of imitative, symbolic, and conceptual factors, all of which necessarily present themselves differently in different periods, cultures, traditions, languages, and families. Which means that when it comes to reading scripture, even if we knew the exact word or phrase that any one of the biblical writers used, there is little chance that strict, definitive meanings from *their* day could be imported into exact understandings of *our* day. Insisting otherwise would be like using bronze-age tools to work out digital-age problems.

Words are fluid. They must be, for their definitions are filtered through the relationship of language and culture, neither of which are static. However, the capital-W Word, filtered through truth and spirit, is also fluid. Sometimes, the Word gets lost in the lowercase -w words, but if we're aware, discerning, vulnerable, and courageous, we might gain the wisdom to see the capital-W Word transcending and including the lowercase-w words.

In case I'm being too poetic, let me be clear: the hope of scripture (lowercase-w words) is the way all of this plays out within the life of Jesus, the Christ (the capital-W Word). Embodied love is the fulfillment of our text. The strength of what the bible offers is not definitive rigidity around rules; the strength is the way words and stories get inside, influence, and then work their way out into healthy, interrelated lives. I name this love, and I'm in agreement with the Apostle Paul who once wrote to his Galatian friends and said, "The only thing that matters is faith expressing itself in love."

A Working Definition of Love

I don't have the final word, but my working definition of love is that it is an uncontrolling, nonbinary, nonviolent, non-scapegoating energy entangled with

God and everyone that's meant for the non-complete flourishing of everything.

- Uncontrolling because if something controls, I find it difficult to call it love.

- Nonbinary because love isn't interested in pitting one thing against another.

- Nonviolent because violence probably isn't love.

- Non-scapegoating because I've come to believe that much religion is built upon a mechanism of blame. I'd like to distance myself from the practice.

- Energy because love isn't exactly a person or a thing.

- Entangled because where God ends, and creation begins is impossible to determine.

- The flourishing of everything because love is so creative that it can lift one thing up without tearing another thing down.

- Non-complete flourishing because I don't think the point of love is to provide wholeness to the degree that you no longer have desire. Desire doesn't work that way. Wanting is fueled by the not-having. It's the lack that produces the energy. So, flourishing isn't necessarily completeness or filling the lack with anything (including with God) so that you are whole. No, the depth of flourishing allows lack to be with you on the journey of love.

I Believe in You

So, this is an approach that encourages you, the reader, the human being, the person privileged to be the steward of this lived experience to choose a lens of love. (An uncontrolling, nonbinary, nonviolent, non-scapegoating energy entangled with God and everyone that's meant for the non-complete flourishing of everything.)

"Wait," I hear you asking, "can I do that?"

Yes! Yes, you can. Love *wants* you to think through these things for yourself. Notice the words of Jesus in Luke 8:18: "consider carefully how you listen."

Look, you already have a context. But this doesn't mean you can't *influence* your context. I know such an idea might cause you anxiety, particularly if you're coming from a religious system that's told you you're incapable of determining your own ideas; that's conditioned you from day one to believe that your heart is "deceitful above all things." But consider that this kind of message has come to you within a certain environment (again, context). Meanwhile, you are free to form your own opinions.

I want to tell you the same thing I told three young women recently at a coffee shop who were probably around the age of my daughter. I couldn't help but notice, as they sat next to me praying, discussing, and drinking coffee, that next to their bibles was a book by a well-known preacher, someone who has made a living off telling young women, just like them, that they cannot lead, teach, or preach, at least, not when men are present.

I cringed, turned the music in my headphones up, and did my best not to think about their limited context. My distraction strategy didn't work. I kept thinking about these young women, their future, *everyone's* future. About an hour later, on my way out, I did my best to respectfully offer my opinion: "Despite what the author of the book you're reading thinks," I said, taking the time to look each of them in the eye, "I believe in you."

And that's what I want to say to you. You are capable and strong. You're empowered and free. You have permission to co-partner with the divine to figure out how to grow and make your best judgment about everything, especially the way scripture will inform your theology. You can't control the lens, but you can *shape* the lens, and what better way to shape than with love? So, yes, bring love into the reading of the text. Watch how it influences your understanding.

- Love with you in Joshua 6, as God commands Joshua to kill every man, woman, child, cow, sheep, and donkey. How do you think love wants you to interpret such a command?

- Love with you in John 8, when the religious leaders, preaching holiness, rules, and consequences, drag the woman caught in adultery to Jesus. What is love asking you when Jesus says, "Let him without sin throw the first stone?"

- And love with you throughout the Book of Revelation, as you read about a quasi-religious imperialistic government marking people in a particular way. Is love saying anything about the way quasi-christian, neo-imperialism has marked you?

Years of reading and studying, thinking and praying, talking with lay people and scholars, writing books and getting degrees have led me to believe the following: One can utilize the bible to get to messages about love, or one can utilize love to get to messages in the bible. I choose the latter.

Whoever has an ear to hear, let them hear.

My Context

Speaking of contexts, mine has been marked by two distinct but overlapping paradigms in the midst of my lived experience. Each of these has played and continues to play a significant role in the shaping and influencing of my story.

Open and Relational Theology

Open and relational theology, a phrase coined by Thomas Jay Oord, (c4ort.org), rallies around two ideas:

First, that God experiences time moment by moment, the result of which is an undetermined future (i.e., open). The future has not yet happened, so it is, unknowable. An open view rejects the notion of a

God with exhaustive divine foreknowledge of all future events. This doesn't mean that God isn't aware of patterns or have good ideas of how things are going to play out, but fixed outcomes make little sense if God is love.

Second, that God is deeply interconnected with creation (i.e., relational). The fundamental building block of all creation, from the micro to the macro, is not independent and substance-based; rather, it is interdependent and relationship-based. This is true of the cosmos and, again, of God. Therefore, a relational view rejects the notion of a God that's separate, unable to experience, and impervious to change. Whatever God is, S(H)e is dynamic, interactive, experiential, and intimately related to all creation. Separateness makes little sense if God is love.

Mimetic Theory

René Girard's (zhee-RAHRD) mimetic theory resists neat summarization, but since it would make little sense for me to talk about my context, without mentioning the theory, I'll offer the briefest of explanations:

Mimetic theory explores how our desires are shaped through relationship and imitation of others, how those desires can become rivalrous and generate conflict, and how this process drives us toward scapegoating as a remedy. Unfortunately, scapegoating works, in fact, it works so well that we've relied on it repeatedly over the millennia, and it's in this repetition that Girard (sees religion being born. As challenging and pessimistic as this all is, for the christian, there may be hope, for there is a way to understand that what Jesus was doing was to become a scapegoat to reveal our addiction to scapegoating religion and to subvert the whole mechanism from the inside out. And I suspect that *is* what has happened.

You can learn about both open and relational theology and mimetic theory in one book, by reading *Theology of Consent: Mimetic Theory in an Open and Relational Universe.*

My Lived Experience with Three Inciting Incidents

As important as both those ideas have been, it's possible that neither of them would have been that interesting to me if my life had gone in a different direction. But my lived experience has shaped me profoundly, particularly those events that I sometimes refer to as "inciting incidents."

An inciting incident is a literary phrase—a way to characterize how tension provides "traction" in a story, propelling it forward toward resolution. Here are three inciting incidents that have shaped and continue to shape my story:

First, I kept meeting people who were not only different from me; they were different from what the church system normally produced. Of course, any system that wishes to exist must produce and reproduce people who fit well within their system. This isn't all that surprising or concerning. What's concerning is how the church system tends to do this in the name of God.

Therefore, if a church system isn't careful, or refuses to listen to outside voices, or lacks awareness of the powerless, it will send the message that Godly people tend to vote the same, express themselves sexually in similar ways, occupy the same social-economic standing, and generally believe all the same kinds of things.

But I kept meeting real, live human beings that didn't fit the mold. Even more, I discovered that many of these outside-the-mold people were genuine, intelligent, and really thoughtful. Each interaction made it increasingly clear that what we held in common was greater than what we didn't. People would leave my

My Context

office, and in so many words, I would think, "Oh, gosh, I think that person who doesn't fit my system is more put together than most of the people I know who *do* fit the system!"

Meanwhile, irrespective of differences, what I intuited time and time again was that unconditional and uncontrolling love was for these people just as much as it was for me.

A second category of inciting incident had to do with the inconsistencies I kept encountering within the sacred text. After a while, I could no longer live in denial about a handful of inconsistencies:

- Sometimes, these issues were something like a science problem. (Wait, archeologists haven't found evidence to support all the details of Israel's journey into the Promised Land? Wait, evolution doesn't rule out the possibility of love and, therefore, the possibility of the divine? God and evolution can co-exist?)

- Sometimes, the issues were anachronistic in that they had to do with how events were presented one way, only to be presented another way in a later passage. (Wait, so in Chronicles, it's Satan that tempts David, but when the same story is told in Samuel, it's Yahweh? Hold on, in Mark's account of the resurrection, it was a young man in white appearing to three women, but in Matthew's account, it was an angel appearing to only one woman?)

- Some of my issues had to do with the difficulty of translation itself. I began recognizing that even within my lifetime, the meaning of certain words had changed or were changing. As I considered translating texts over 2,500 years, in some cases from languages that were no longer even used, and I considered changing customs, traditions, and cultural shifts, I knew it was no longer reasonable to expect any modern-day bible to be 100% error-free. (Time out, the Greek word *metanoia* means change your way of thinking rather than repent? And the Hebrew name *El Shaddai* means "I am the breasted God" and not The Almighty?)

- And finally, some of my problems had to do with the reality of incompatible messaging. (Let me get this straight, in the very same passage that people were told to stone gay people, they were also told to love their neighbor. How does that work? What do you do if your neighbor is gay? How do you stay biblical and love your neighbor but stay biblical and stone your neighbor?)

Some inconsistencies were more acute than others, but the point is, all of these and many others served to catalyze questions.

The well-intentioned bible-loving christian often respond to these questions in the only way they know how, which is to flatly quote 2Timothy 3:16 and assert that "ALL scripture is inspired." But, even if we ignored the circular logic employed by using the text to say that the text is inspired, you should still be aware that at the time Timothy was reading that line, the only existing scriptures were the first five books of the Old Testament and writing from the prophets.

The entirety of what the Protestant-West now calls the bible, wasn't ratified for *another 300+ years.* During that time, the fight over which books would and would not be thought of as "inspired" was intense, full of disagreement, banishments, and excommunications. And since that time? Good grief, look at history. Debates about how to think of scripture have launched a thousand book burnings, excommunications, skirmishes, and wars.

Whatever else is going on with "inspired scripture," the text itself doesn't need to be thought of as infallible, inerrant, or without error. Such thinking only opens the door to the previously mentioned insanity.

There are healthier moves to make with the concept of "inspired." Here are three:

1. It's inspired to help the reader see the stupidity of trying to establish power by way of words, *particularly when the words talk so much about love.*

2. It's inspired to help the reader see that using certain passages about grace to decode other passages about violence is an intelligent move.

3. What the bible is inspired to do is help the reader be introduced to an *inspired messiah.*

My third category of inciting incident can be summed up with one word: loss. There are too many to list here, and I write about grief more in my book *indigo: the color of grief,* but sicknesses, fires, the loss of denominational estimation (in official and unofficial ways), tragedies, car wrecks, and the deaths of multiple family members—sometimes under violent and absurd situations—all impacted the way I engaged with theology and scripture. Loss changed me in many ways, not least in that it left me feeling powerless.

Being out of power not only destabilized the way I related to God and the way I read scripture, it also altered the way I related to others who had experience with loss. I don't mean to suggest that a straight, white, American, relatively affluent and educated, christian male—someone who obviously checks all the power boxes—can completely relate to the Native American, the trafficked, the queer, the families forever changed by slavery, the women, the divorced, the migrant, the abused, or any number of other individuals and people groups who have suffered.

I'm uninterested in appropriating their pain; however, if my loss has done anything for me, it's helped me see how powerlessness, in general, can inform one's theology in powerful ways.

Now You Know

So, now you know a bit about what I've been through. It's important, particularly as I'm trying to help you begin to work through theological issues, that I'm honest about what I've been through and how it motivated me in my theological studies. All of this (and more) has contributed to why I've shaped the lens through which I interpret life, as best I can, into a lens of love.

I've tried other approaches, but none have provided much life, at least not for long. Take your pick: a doubling down on holiness living, deference to denomination, confession of creeds, bible memorization, church attendance, giving large percentages of my income away, going on missions trips, not to mention rooting out all immorality by going through long seasons of "taking every thought captive." (Ha, that last one can sure take some time.) None of that has really helped me all that much, and much of it left me feeling a bit helpless. The thing that *has* brought hope, really, genuinely, is love.

If you're uninterested in love, fair enough. If that's the case, then the micro-theology series, influenced as it is by open and relational thinking, probably isn't for you. However, if you're sensing an invitation to cultivate a new approach—one that's creative, open-ended, and inclusive, which both requires *and* increases intellectual honesty, then maybe this will be the start of something new for you.

I hope so.

Love Burns Like Fire: An Open and Relational Take on Hell

What Is Chunking and What Does It Have to Do with Thoughts on Hell?

The word "chunk" is used differently by various psychologists and scientists. It can be a noun or a verb, as something one does consciously or subconsciously and any of these ideas might apply to how I'm using it in this writing. To keep information organized while formulating new ways of thinking, our brains break down big ideas into manageable chunks. Without this ability, it wouldn't take much to get overwhelmed with all the data. As one walks through an entrance to a maze that itself leads to an entire garden, so chunking acts like walking through doorways that lead into entire gardens of thought.

The point of this writing is not to flood you with all the garden knowledge I have (honestly, there are a lot of weeds in the garden so you don't want all of it anyhow) but instead to give the chunks that over the course of about two years, allowed a whole new way of thinking to open up for me. Don't be misled by each point's brevity, for it might have taken me hours, sometimes months and years, of reading, thinking, and reflecting to boil some of these ideas down to a sentence or two. And thank God I *did* gain a whole new way of thinking because, it gave me a new way to keep the idea of love at play whenever I interacted with the idea of hell.

Never Abandoned by Love

Let me put it this way . . . despite the massive loss (and losses) I had experienced, I never got the sense that love had abandoned me. I got the sense that something had abandoned me, and at times, it certainly felt like God, but once I reworked expansive and non-sacrificial ideas of love into my imagination, I started thinking, "Oh, maybe that old thing wasn't really God."

Furthermore, keeping love at play, even in discussions about hell, gave me just enough freedom to say that everything might be thought of in light of a movement that was redemptive and good. I mean, given love's faithfulness in the past, it's not a stretch to say that love will be faithful in the future.

Much of my work had to do with disassembling and reassembling the concept of love itself. And as I mentioned in the introduction, my concept was run and re-run through a matrix of mimetic theory, open and relational theology, and my lived experience as a father to the point that I began thinking of it differently than I previously had thought of it. Interestingly enough, I started chunking the definition of love itself into the following thought:

Love is an uncontrolling, non-violent, non-binary, non-scapegoating energy in relationship with God and the world that's meant for the non-complete flourishing of everyone and everything.

And chunking God that way—ha, which sounds like a weird phrase—allowed me to deconstruct the narrative that I had inherited from

Americanized-christianity regarding a lot of things, not least of which is the topic of punishment and hell.

It's funny; the chunks came to me, in a way, as my own, and yet, I am deeply indebted to dozens of thinkers, poets, and writers for helping me get there. As the poet Lee Welch puts it . . .

Like everything else I have,
somebody showed it to me,
and I found it all by myself.

I Changed My Mind About Hell When I Realized . . .

1. **that** being merciful takes more strength than being judgmental.

2. **how** many "loving people" were upset over my refusal to condemn certain people to a place devoid of love.

3. **that** the main Greek and Hebrew terms Sheol (SHEE-ole), Hades (HAY-deez), Gehenna (geh-HEN-nah), and Tartarus (TAR-tar-us) used in the bible were not equal to the English word "hell" with its punitive-judgment-eternal-flames-never-quench God's-burning-wrath meaning.

4. **even** more, despite the different and sometimes contrasting terms from which we get the English word "hell," that the biblical writers all shared a common denominator: a potential end (which is, in and of itself, a serious challenge to Americanized-christianity's presuppositions about divine punishment.)

5. **that** if I got to heaven but learned a family member, say a child, was in hell . . . not only would I NOT worship God all the more, as I had heard some preach . . . I wouldn't even stay. You think I'm sticking around heaven in that kind of scenario? No, man, saddle the horses; I'm going after my kid.

6. **I** couldn't imagine any God-forsaken space in the entire cosmos.

7. **that** yes, judgment is real, but the judgment is *love*. Despite what people were telling me, I knew this wasn't a cop-out because sometimes love is incredibly challenging and painful.

8. **the** literalists were obsessed with reading punishment, wrath, and fire as literal and love as metaphorical vs. *the other way around*, and I thought, "Well, that's wrong."

9. **That** if fire is involved, it'd be good to keep Song of Solomon 8:6 in mind: "Love burns like fire, the brightest kind of flame.

10. **that** I'd never torture my kid once, let alone for eternity. Why would I imagine God doing such a thing?

11. **that** in The Prodigal Son story, the one in the worst shape is the older brother, who represents the religious crowd.

12. **that** religious people (my people) are usually the last to get it: to believe that those who don't think like us are going to hell after they die is to be living in a type of hell while we are alive.

13. **that** if "every knee bows and every tongue confesses," it won't be out of coercive fear. It'll be that love—maybe like the weightiest gravity—just makes it so easy to bow and confess. I mean, could it even be called love if coercive fear is involved?

14. **how** ridiculous it would be for God to command us to love our enemies while he punished his.

15. **after** looking into passages like Romans 1, that there is a healthier, more interesting, if not biblical, way to interpret wrath. I got this idea from

Bradley Jersak, but wrath can be seen as "God's divine consent to our self-destructive choices." It's a much more robust idea than God simply being angry about our behavior.

16. **Gehenna**, which translators historically rendered as 'hell,' was actually a cursed valley beyond Jerusalem's walls. This was where kings, both foreign and Jewish, sacrificed children to satisfy their gods. Holding this image alongside the doctrine of Penal Substitutionary Atonement—the story of a son who was sacrificed outside Jerusalem's walls to satisfy God's wrath—gave me reason to pause.

17. **that** the biblical writers shared no unified concept of hell, drawing instead from diverse metaphors—laundry tubs, refiner's fire, garbage dumps, dungeons, darkness, and sulfurous lakes. They envisioned various scenarios: purgatory-like states, annihilation where people ceased to exist, and importantly, situations where divine love never relented, eventually allowing the outcast to enter heaven's gates.

18. **after** reading The Great Divorce by C.S. Lewis that hell could be an experience we have due to

our own choosing. (Also, I realized that the evangelicals who seemed to love Lewis had either never *read* The Great Divorce or had *ignored* what he wrote because it contradicted so much of what they taught about divine punishment.)

19. that early church fathers like Origen, Clement, Basil, and Gregory all taught a type of universalism.

20. there might be hope for some beyond this life because the crucifixion-resurrection story contained an *in-between part* where Jesus preached good news in the land of the dead.

21. that at the end of Scripture, Jesus says he is making all things new, which doesn›t necessarily do away with punishment, *per se*, but it does give us hope that something good might still be recycled out of all the pain.

22. that the gates of heaven, as John the Revelator tells it, will never be shut.

23. I was more interested in a God who liked the outsiders as much as the insiders.

24. that love running out of patience was anti-biblical.

25. that while our regular, old inferior human-justice system would never suggest that severe punishments be the right move for minor infractions, popular conceptions of divine justice often seemed to operate by completely different standards.

26. that the concept of an "age of accountability"—where children become spiritually responsible for their sins at a certain age and then face eternal punishment if they don't choose correctly—is absurd. What would that age even be? If we say seven, or nine, or 24, good Lord, what about the seven, nine, or 24-year-old who's been manipulated, abused, or trafficked? Surely there would need to be some qualification around such a pronouncement on the young person for all eternity. And surely, we could recognize that once we start down this path, that there would be no way—zero chance—that we could ever figure out where to stop making qualifications. This one idea, alone, influences *everything* Americanized-christianity has to say about the concept of hell.

27. that a God of non-violence is way more compelling than a God of violence. This was true when I examined three key stories I'd inherited:

First, that the origin story I had inherited, which essentially told me that for God to create, he had to descend from somewhere else to dominate and conquer the immoral, amorphous chaos . . .

Second, that the atonement story I had inherited, which basically told me that for God to forgive, he had to have a perfect sacrifice killed and offered to him . . .

And third, that the future-justice-project God was ushering in that I had inherited, which, more or less, told me that for restoration, God would have to violently destroy evil and anyone associated.

All of these seemed to be responses that put our ultimate hope in violence more than love, and though I couldn't deny that there were some injustices I personally wanted to end—violently or not—I just thought a non-violent God was more compelling.

28. that restorative justice is greater than retributive justice, which really isn't justice at all. Look, any God can punish, but it takes a *real* God to redeem, restore, and put people on the path of justice. Justice is probably the depth of what needs to be wrestled with when it comes to any discussions about heaven, hell, punishment, and hope for the future.

Let me share something personal and difficult about my sister . . .

At one level, I'm glad that the one who perpetrated a violent crime against my sister is behind bars, but at another level, I admit, it does nothing for my sister. It does keep the person from doing something similar to someone else, and that, of course, is important. But it does nothing for my sister. Irrespective of how much or how long the criminal is punished, she is never coming home again.

However, suppose the story of restorative justice is true; that there's an experience beyond this life where the unjust go through the fire of God's love. In that case, eventually, there's a chance that the criminal might genuinely ask for forgiveness of my sister . . . her parents, family, God, and the whole universe . . . and in doing so, will unclench his hold on violence, which, in turn, will unclench the hold violence has had on him.

This unclenching would obviously be good for the criminal, but here's the thing . . . it'd be good for all of us. Trust me, I do not ask such things lightly, but what's going to mend such a violent rupture as murder? Enforced incarceration for all eternity or giving someone a chance to own his crime and genuinely ask for forgiveness? As challenging as all this is, I think it's the latter.

Take My Punishment

Well, there you go . . . 28 ways I chunked my way out of hell and started helping others do the same. As I said, each one of them could be "double-clicked" and their implications considered at length.

Of course, after I began sharing these, the real work began because people started pointing fingers (literally) and saying that by believing this way meant I was the one in danger of going to hell. Which was odd because I had just finished telling them that I didn't really believe in the place they were now saying I would go.

Ha! Over the years, I've learned to respond the best I can, which usually involves me taking a breath and saying something like, "You know, if I'm sent to hell over my insistence . . .

- that mercy is greater than sacrifice,

- that love is more enduring than fear,

- and that good fathers always welcome their children home?

Then so be it. I'll take my punishment."

Some Comments from the Original Essay on Substack/Patreon

Note: This includes some, but not all, of the comments. Also, I made minor alterations to a few words both to try and help narrators for the audio version and to accommodate the book's organization into 28 chunks rather than the 24 that are online.

 Reader Comment 1

What an interesting read. It felt (to me) like following Divine breadcrumbs. And it feels delightful to me whenever I hear (or read about) someone else recognizing change happening. It's like reality opening so we can see more than we even knew we were capable. It also feels to me like whatever was covering my/our eyes falls away bit by bit so that we see more clearly. And I feel like this is true for the heart too that whatever has covered my/our heart from past experiences can drop away so we feel more love in ways we never knew was possible—as Love Itself loving through me/us.

I freely admit, I had to look up who Lee Welch is because I loved the quote you shared of his. It feels like he speaks my language (LOL) or I speak his?

Like everything else I have,
somebody showed it to me,
and I found it all by myself.

> **jonathan_foster Response**
>
> Divine breadcrumbs is a great metaphor... it is a bit like that, isn't it? Honestly, i had to look him up as well, and i'm still not sure i found the right person. I've had that quote in my phone for months though. It's so insightful.
>
> I love that you wrote the following... "that whatever has covered my/our heart from past experiences can drop away so we feel more

> love in ways we never knew was possible—as
> Love Itself loving through me/us."
>
> Yes and thank you.

Reader Comment 2

The concept of hell only makes sense within an unscientific cosmology that was the standard of the writers of the Bible. Modern astronomical discoveries make the concept of hell ridiculous. Paul says that the body that survives death is a spiritual one. This raises the question: How do you burn a spiritual body? The Bible also teaches, or at least the creeds dictate, that there will be a resurrection of the physical body. If that is the case, where will the body reside after death, either in heaven or in hell? None of these ideas make any sense when we start asking serious questions.

The best way to dispatch the idea of hell is to dispense with the idea of God altogether, at least the Biblical idea of God. Christians are taught that God is the same throughout the Bible, but a close and critical reading will reveal that the concept of God changes over time, just as the picture of Jesus is different across the four gospels and Paul's authentic epistles and those fraudulent ones attributed to Paul. Reason makes the concepts of a Biblical God, heaven, hell, eternal punishment, etc., illogical and untenable in light of Biblical scholarship, archaeological evidence, and modern cosmological discoveries. We can try to weave and dance around the ideas that God is more about love than wrath, but the truth is that he is both, and many other emotions.

The Bible says that we are made in the image of God. Someone has said that it is more likely that God is made in the image of us. So if we believe that God and heaven and hell are human constructs that emerged from the human mind, then we can erase these constructs from the human mind and live a life based on human constructs such as love and respect and concern and cooperation and kindness, all freely given without any religious coercion such as heaven and hell.

> **jonathan_foster Response**
>
> Thanks for your comments . . .
>
> First, you might be right . . . it's possible that it might be better to throw the whole thing out!
>
> Second, I agree with some of what I hear you saying . . . specifically, the part about how we're

taught that God is the same vs. the concept of God changing. What I think I think is that God does change. If God is love, then change is necessary because when you love someone, you will be changed! That's just the way it works.

Third, just for fun, and not for arguing, let me offer something that might be a bit science and a bit faith (as I think that both science and faith are very much a part of the lived human experience)

The science part would have to do with evolution. It is reality, although I've come to realize that while evolution and survival of the fittest is a great answer as to what is going on, it's not a great answer as to why it's going on. "Survival" is not the same as "arrival" and arrival has to do with adaptation, change, movement and complexification (though, yes, there's also a lot of entropy).

The faith part would have to do with the why . . . why the forward-movement-complexity thing? Nobody really knows, but lots of reasonably intelligent thinkers propose the idea of something existing beyond our senses being responsible. I don't know for sure, but I suspect that that something might be love.

Meanwhile, I think there's a possibility that God herself just might be love. Not a hallmark, kitcshy, christian-radio, pop-song kinda love, but something much, much more interesting, robust, and compelling. And I think that there's a biblical way to read all of God's attribute emanating from love; rather, than love simply being one of God's emotional attributes.

And if that is true ... then I'm interested in keeping God around and think that the whole idea might give us reason to evolve beyond who we currently are as a species.

ha, or i could be wrong! Thanks for your comments.

 Reader Comment 3

The scripture says that God is love. Why not turn it around and love is God. Is that sort of what you are saying? No doubt we can learn much from the Bible about love and kindness. It's just that I think we can do this as humans without the encumbrances that come with the involvement of the word God. Why is love not enough without it having to be entangled with all the mystical and inexplicable mysteries that pertain to a concept of God, especially the Christian concept? I appreciate your journey and the writing you do. Thanks for moving and not standing still in your quest. Peace ✌.

> ☞ **jonathan_foster Response**
>
> Yes, that's what I'm saying . . .
>
> and I'm with you on the encumbrance part . . .
>
> and i hear you on "why isn't love enough without the entanglement with all the mystical stuff . . ." Hmm . . . i think feel some compassion for people who I know will never be able to lay all the mystical stuff aside. So I guess I feel a sense of responsibility to let them know that there are healthier ways to approach the Bible or the mysthcal. But honestly, I don't really disagree with a lot of what you're saying! Thnx
>
> Weird, I woke up this morning, some four months removed from this comment thinking I'm not quite comfortable with leaving it at "since God is love then love is God." So, yes, God

is love, but it doesn't entirely work to say love is God.

I think I think this way, because the two direct, unqualified declarative statements about God's essence in Scripture are God is love and God is spirit. Therefore, to say "love is God" feels overly reductionist.

It might leave some interesting stuff out. For example, saying God is Spirit reinforces the idea of omnipresence, which I think is very important.

Also, the Hebrew and Greek terms most often used in the Bible are *Ruach* and *Pneuma*. These can be interpreted as wind or breath. There's something about the active (albeit invisible) way wind and breath operate in the world that helps me think in terms of an active, living God.

Furthermore, Spirit can mean something like mind or intention. So, maybe what I think is that God is a universal Spirit with an intention of love (the kind of love as I've mentioned in other places that is an uncontrolling, non-violent, non-binary, non-scapegoating energy in relationship with God and the whole world, meant for the non-complete flourishing of everyone and everything.)

And now that I'm thinking about it, though this one needs more time to unpack when the philosopher Hegel talks about spirit (Geist) he's talking about a capacity of thought to apprehend contradiction rather than be defeated by it. And I think this idea of contradiction plays a role with the "non-complete flourishing" that I included in my definition of love.

Of course, for you, much of my response doesn't matter because you're already intuiting some things without the "encumbrances that come with the involvement of the word God." And I respect that, so maybe this will be for anyone else who reads this.

Or, ha, maybe it's just for me.

Reader Comment 4

Do these 24 points come as a result of you wanting to be faithful to the Bible, or as a result of being willing to set some parts of it aside? (Genuine question, not sarcastic.

This is just the first of your posts that I've ever come across.)

> **jonathan_foster Response**
>
> Good question . . . Very much attempting to be faithful in reading the Bible well.
>
> **Reader Comment 4a**
>
> Good to hear. I don't agree that you have been faithful to the Bible, but I'm glad to hear that's your aim, and this probably isn't the forum for in depth discussion.
>
> **jonathan_foster Response**
>
> You're welcome to ask a question, but no problem if you'd rather not. Either way, all my best.
>
> **Reader Comment 4b**
>
> I'm hesitant, just because it's a tricky topic and an online discussion. One comment is that I think point #12 represents either a significant misunderstanding of other people's views or a significant misunderstanding of the gospel itself.

 jonathan_foster Response

I respect the hesitancy. Regarding: #12 . . . bout already being in a type of hell if we think others are going there who don't think like us?

Hmm, upon re-reading, I think the logic is sound IF the Christian makes the gospel a reductionistic move . . . that is, boils everything down to whether someone prays the right prayer and confesses the right confession so as to go to heaven rather than hell upon cessation of breathing . . . the very thing (in my lived experience) much Christian theology does.

But if the gospel is more expansive, well, among other things, then those who live in alignment with its expansiveness won't have any need of such thinking.

Does that help? And no pressure to get into it here. I agree with you . . . online stuff can be crazy sometimes. peace.

Reader Comment 4c

Thanks for the thoughts. I don't think saying that salvation includes a profession of faith and repentance for your sins (which is exactly what Jesus, Paul, Jonah etc. say is required to avoid punishment) is the same as saying that salvation belongs to those who think a certain way.

I've never heard a single Christian in my life say that people who don't think like them are going to hell. Maybe that's because I've been in good churches. If what you mean by "think the same as me" is "profess faith and repentance of their sins", then I don't think that's a problem, so your critique of hell doesn't hold. If you mean something more shallow, then why engage with the shallowest version of what you're arguing against? If you're arguing against hell as a biblical doctrine, surely you want to "steel man" it by refering to biblical teaching, rather than a perversion of the gospel?

👉 jonathan_foster Response

Thanks, appreciate the dialogue . . . I'll try and keep it short . . . i hate that so many words makes it look I'm draggin' on and on . . . ha, but truthfully, these things take some nuance and i'm glad that places like substack and patreon afford us the space.

Regarding: "arguing against hell as a biblical doctrine." That's not really what I'm doing... well, not exactly... So, I'd say something like yes, teaching about hell (or Genehann, Hades, Sheol, and Tarterus) is in the Bible. It definitely needs to be dealt with. A part of what I'm doing in this post is "dealing with it." It's not exhaustive, but it introduces questions/comments into the discussion that might help the reader paint a more in-depth understanding of what the Bible writers could have been getting at when talking about after-life.

Further... to clarify... the bible doesn't really have a doctrine of hell. (Neither do the early creeds). As previous paragraph indicates and indeed, the entire post, the bible has A LOT of thoughts about what might be going on so, using the phrase, "Biblical doctrine of hell" makes it sound like there's this one systemized take in Scripture. And it's just not true. There's a ton of room for interpretation, which btw, is a good thing!

Regarding: "I've never heard a single Christian in my life say that people who don't think like them are going to hell." You are probably right.

And honestly, I've never heard someone utter that phrase exactly either. But, what I'm trying to do is peel back the veneer of theology to the degree that we can see what is going on underneath. And though I haven't heard anyone say that, well, that is what is very much what is going on when, for example, the preacher-friend points his finger at me and says, "It's you and people like you who are responsible for my gay sibling going to hell." This, in response, to my insistence upon acceptance of gay people.

Regarding: "faith and repentance of sins . . ." Hmmm, yes, you might be right. I do think faith and repentance of sins is important. Of course, the problem is always . . . what constitutes sin? And in discussions about after-life, is there a chance for sin to be forgiven there? Oh, and what constitutes repentance? Is it a prayer? Is it a way of life? Personally, I'm down with both! But, lots and lots of different theological takes will go in different directions here. (and germane to the point . . . if I don't agree with them, they are prone to say that I'm wrong and in danger of being punished in the afterlife!)

Regarding: "Why engage with the shallowest version of what you are arguing against?" This is a good critique because yes, in a sense, point #12 is a reaction against a shallow version of hell. And as such, people should just skip over it if it's not helpful. Hmm, however, I think I want to say something like . . .

For me, if each of these 28 points (and many others that I didn't include) represent a light in the sky . . . one could connect the lights and see a certain kind of constellation forming. If you pull out the weakest lights (which, in this case for you would be #12) you would STILL have a compelling constellation to consider . . . one that, in many ways, disagrees with what Americanized-christianity has been talking about for the last couple hundred years that I think is damaging, unhelpful, and in the end, counter to the biblical trajectory of love, mercy, and grace.

But I'm fine with someone not seeing some of the lights . . . of forming a different constellation . . . I would never dare to imagine that everyone would agree with everything I'm saying here; however, I know that if one finds resonance with a lot of it, well, it'll still be a very interesting image in the night sky and ultimately, will change their posture toward all of this.

Thanks again for the comments and questions. All my best.

 Reader Comment 4d

Thanks for these thoughts Jonathan. I appreciate you clarifying what you're aiming to do here. As you said, we see the "constellation" differently, but thanks for the dialogue.

 Reader Comment 5

Thank you for this read. I read it first in my email this morning, then clicked over to Substack and parsed through it again. Over the years, being away from the christian bubble that I grew up in, I have finally shed my fear (or joy) of any such place as hell or a heaven. I don't think either of those supernatural planes of supposed existence that we were indoctrinated with make any sense or have any evidence to support them. But I'm not here to troll your post, I simply just want to say what ultimately put it all to bed for me was the concept of TIME.

Some Comments from the Original Essay

It's difficult, albeit impossible(?) to talk about existence outside of time... because ultimately our existence is dependent on a time-based system. We of course invented this concept in order to make sense of that reality, so do with that knowledge as you will. But as a young adult, I started to put extra "time" into studying the concept, and thinking about what "outside of time" really meant... or more specifically, what "forever" meant. How do you actually calculate infinity?

And of course you can wrap your mind in circles on the scientific methodological behind infinity, what it actually means, where we think it leads, etc. But in the sense of said indoctrination, it was always framed as we would be "rejoicing in Heaven with our God forever"... or we would be "burning in a lake of fire after the judgement... again... forever".

My 20 something mind started to wonder... does that sound like joy... does that sound threatening? When you burn something... the very definition of burning is changing one form of energy into another form... solids into a gas. In the case of burning forever... that doesn't mean much to me. Physics are what... suspended... and you scream out in pain more than a few minutes before what... you never passing out... all without time? This doesn't really compute.

> On the flip side ... same scenario: you wake up in heaven, rejoicing, angels are singing, streets of gold, all the metaphors. But like you said above, you DO or DO NOT realize that your loved ones are there? Do ... or CAN you feel happy or sad about that? Supposedly there are no tears ... right? So, it would seem that you can't be sad about not having your loved one's there, so what does that say about your awareness of what is even happening? And then to bring back my own point, you sing a physical sound from your lungs, mouth, from a tongue?? And you sing forever? What? Again ... that doesn't make any sense ... all music is time based ... how you would know the beat, how would you hear the pitch? I'm a musician, so I understand how music works, and music as far as I know is a time based element that makes it work through and through.

"Forever" or "Infinity" is the same as saying "something happens for zero amount of time" ... which is to ultimately say: This doesn't happen. Therefore ... I just don't believe it's real.

Thanks for coming to my Ted Talk. LOL.

Once again... not trolling... I really enjoy your posts. I'm probably going to use this commentary for my own post today. Would you mind if I linked to your story here, and show my response? Thanks.

>  **jonathan_foster Response**
>
> Thanks.
>
> Re: time... ha, it's so frustrating how complicated the subject matter gets so quickly. But I don't think I disagree with anything that you say here. And as you may have noticed, I didn't put anything about my thoughts on the concept of "eternal" or "forever." I'm not really sure what I think because I recognize that my entire concept of beauty hinges directly upon the reality that nothing lasts forever.
>
> Re: change, time, and physics... yes, exactly. Your point is well taken. And whether from the internalist crowd or the universalist crowd... neither party seems to do much exploration around change, which for me has everything to do with everything being relational, and absolutely presupposes time.

I'm thankful you've been able to shed the weight of expectation (that you call fear or joy) about any of this. I think there's something really beautiful about humans being able to live in the present and not get consumed with what's going to happen in the future, let alone with such speculative ideas as I'm bringing up here. (And ironically, there is something joyful, maybe even heaven-like about living that way.)

Thnx for the comments and no, i didn't take it as trolling at all!

A Few Resources

Deconstructing Hell: Open and Relational Responses to the Doctrine of Eternal Conscious Torment, Chad Bahl, 2023, SacraSage Press

Facing Apocalypse: Climate, Democracy, and Other Last Chances, Catherine Keller, 2021, Orbis Books

Her Gates Will Never Be Shut: Hope, Hell, and the New Jerusalem, Bradley Jersak, 2009, Wipf & Stock Publishers

Razing Hell: Rethinking Everything You've Been Taught about God's Wrath and Judgment, Sharon L. Baker, 2010, Westminster John Knox Press

Reading Revelation Responsibly: Uncivil Worship and Witness: Following the Lamb into the New Creation, Michael J. Gorman, 2011, Wipf & Stock Publishers

Reversed Thunder: The Revelation of John and the Praying Imagination, Eugene H. Peterson, 1988, HarperCollins Publishers

The Suffering of God: An Old Testament Perspective, Terence E. Fretheim, 1984, Fortress Press

That All Shall Be Saved: Heaven, Hell, and Universal Salvation, David Bentley Hart, 2019, Yale University Press

The Uncontrolling Love of God: An Open and Relational Account of Providence, Thomas Jay Oord, 2015, IVP Academic

About the Author

Jonathan J. Foster is the partner of one, father of three, author, podcaster, co-founder and chief advocate for LoveHaiti.org. He holds a doctorate in theology from Northwind Seminary and leads OpenTable.Network, a new denominational organization empowering faith communities, pastors, chaplains, and spiritual directors in their local, missional context.

Other Books by Jonathan J. Foster

- *indigo: the color of grief*, SacraSage Press, 2024

- *Theology of Consent: Mimetic Theory in an Open and Relational Universe*, SacraSage Press, 2023

- *The Reconstructionist: Mercy>Sacrifice, People>Text, Love>Fear*, Quoir Publishing, 2022
- *Questions About Sexuality that Got Me Uninvited from My Denomination*, Verde Group, 2019

Some Other Books in the Micro Theology Series

Book 1
At-One-Ment: An Open and Relational Take on Atonement

Book 2
Love Burns like Fire: An Open and Relational Take on Hell

Book 3
Centers in the Hands of an Edgy God: An Open and Relational Take on Eschatology

Book 4
Hidden in Plain Sight: An Open and Relational Take on Sexuality

AI Disclosure

If you're looking for AI-generated writing, you're in the wrong place. My writing will always be my own work. Yes, of course, I do use software like Grammarly for copyediting—it's incredibly helpful, though, in an effort to preserve my "own voice," I find myself consistently ignoring some of its suggestions. And recently, I started using Claude.ai for some research and ideation, though what it's been most helpful for is formatting (e.g., "Claude, does the flow of my content match my Table of Contents?") So far, Claude.ai doesn't feel all that dissimilar to using a very fast, detailed, if not conversational search engine. Side note: My search engine of choice is Ecosia because, like Claude.ai's parent company, Anthropic, they seem relatively ethical. For good or for bad, friends, *everything* is relative.

ALSO FROM
SacraSage Press...

SACRASAGEPRESS.COM

Made in the USA
Coppell, TX
04 February 2026